REAL
MOMENTS
for
LOVERS

◆

Also by Barbara De Angelis

REAL MOMENTS

ARE YOU THE ONE FOR ME?

SECRETS ABOUT MEN EVERY WOMAN SHOULD KNOW

HOW TO MAKE LOVE ALL THE TIME

REAL
MOMENTS

for

LOVERS

◆

Barbara De Angelis, Ph.D.

Delacorte  Press

Published by
Delacorte Press
Bantam Doubleday Dell Publishing Group, Inc.
1540 Broadway
New York, New York 10036

Library of Congress Cataloging in Publication Data

De Angelis, Barbara.
    Real moments for lovers / by Barbara De Angelis.
        p.   cm.
    ISBN 0-385-31429-9
    1. Love.   2. Intimacy (Psychology)   3. Interpersonal communication.   4. Sex in marriage.   I. Title.
    BF575.L8D37   1995
    306.7—dc20   94-38438
                                                          CIP

DESIGN: Stanley S. Drate/Folio Graphics Co., Inc.

Manufactured in the United States of America
Published simultaneously in Canada

February 1995

10   9   8   7   6   5   4   3   2   1

For Jeffrey,
my ancient and eternal love

CONTENTS

Part One
✦
DISCOVERING THE SPIRIT
OF LOVE

Part Two
✦
REAL MOMENTS
AND EVERYDAY INTIMACY

Part Three
✦
REAL MOMENTS
AND SEXUAL LOVE

Part One

✦

DISCOVERING THE SPIRIT OF LOVE

1

Why Lovers Need Real Moments

This book is for lovers. It is for lovers who have already found their beloved, and are traveling the path of relationship together. It is for lovers who no longer feel like lovers, and want to rediscover their passionate connection again. And it is for lovers who are alone, waiting to live as the lovers they are meant to be until they meet their heart's true companion.

◆

When you have a lover in your life, you are richly blessed. You have been given the gift of another person who has chosen to walk beside you. He or she will share your days and your nights, your bed and your burdens.

He will see secret parts of you that no one else sees. He will touch places on your body that no one else touches. He will seek you out where you have been hiding and create a safe haven for you within his arms.

Your lover offers you an abundance of miracles every day. He has the power to delight you with his smile, his voice, the scent of his neck, the way he moves. He has the power to banish your loneliness. He has the power to turn the ordinary into the sublime. He is your doorway to Heaven here on Earth.

◆

What does it mean to be a lover? It is more than just being married to someone or making love to him or her. Millions of people are married, millions of people have sex, but few are real lovers.

To be a real lover you must commit to and participate in a perpetual dance of intimacy with your partner.

◆ You are a lover when you appreciate the gift that your partner is, and celebrate that gift every day.

◆ You are a lover when you remember that your partner does not belong to you—*he or she is on loan from the universe, and if you do not take good care of him, you will lose him*—he will leave you emotionally, and maybe even physically.

✦ You are a lover when you realize that nothing that happens between you will be insignificant, that everything you say in the relationship has the potential to cause your beloved joy or sorrow, and everything you do will either strengthen your connection or weaken it.

✦ You are a lover when you understand all this, and thus wake up each morning filled with gratitude that you have another day in which to love and enjoy your partner.

When **hen you and your mate forget that your relationship is a gift, when you don't remember to cherish one another, that's when you cease being lovers.**

I think there's nothing worse than being in a relationship but no longer feeling like lovers. One day, you look at your partner and realize, with a sinking feeling, that "I love him, *but I'm not in love anymore.*" The sacred bridge between your hearts has disappeared, and in its place, you are left with a gnawing emptiness. You may still share a bed, a home, even a family, but you don't share that ecstatic bond that true lovers share. You have become roommates.

Falling out of love and losing that magnetic attraction you once had does not happen overnight. It is simply the inevitable result that occurs when one or both of you take the gift of your partner for granted, when you stop thinking and behaving like lovers.

✦

Why aren't more people lovers, rather than merely husband and wife? Because they don't try hard enough in their relationship to be kind, because they don't remember to look for the true beauty of their partner's spirit, and most of all, *because they don't experience enough real moments together.*

In order to remain lovers, you need real moments in your relationship.

Real moments occur when you and your partner are totally focused on one another and the love between you in the moment, when you are fully experiencing whatever is happening, when you allow your hearts to connect and the feelings to flow freely. You can have a real moment when you're making love, or making breakfast. It's not **what** you're doing that matters—it's **how you pay attention to what you're doing that makes it into a real moment.**

Being a true lover requires that you pay attention to your partner, to the relationship, and to yourself. The problem is that many of us live our emotional lives mindlessly, without thinking, without feeling, automatically and unconsciously. You talk, you embrace, you have sex, but often without paying full attention to what you are doing. You are worrying about the errands you have to run, or remembering the phone calls you haven't returned, or pondering a problem with one of your children, everything but what you should be focused on—loving your partner.

When you don't pay attention to the person you're loving while you're loving him or her, you are somewhere other than in the moment. You're remembering the past or worrying about the future, but you're not right here, right now. When you're not here, you can't truly connect with your lover. He won't be able to feel you. *You* won't be able to feel you. *And when you can't feel yourself fully in the moment, it will be impossible to feel "in love."*

$\mathcal{T}$o feel "in love," you and your
partner must both be in the state of
love
within yourselves.
Only then can you see love in one
another.

When lovers don't share enough real moments with one another, they starve the soul of their relationship. You can spend every minute in each other's presence, but unless you are experiencing some real moments, you won't ever truly be together.

Real moments will teach you how to pay attention with your heart, to start being right here, right now. And it is those real moments that will ultimately give depth and meaning to your relationship, and keep you feeling eternally in love.

Real Moments and Sexual Love

When you have a lover, you share one thing with him or her that, hopefully, you share with no one else, and that is the act of sexual union. Each time you and your beloved unite, you penetrate each other's physical boundaries, and merge not just your hearts but your bodies in the most intimate way possible. I believe, as did many ancient spiritual traditions, *that sex is a sacred force,* for it is through sex that all life begins. Sexual energy, then, is simply the energy of life expressing itself through your body. And when you learn to use that force as a celebration of life and of your relationship, you can turn what is usually mere physical pleasure into physical and emotional ecstasy.

> Sex is a sacred sharing —
> it is the way your spirit
> and the spirit of your beloved
> can dance together in the flesh.

Sex is a physical celebration of the spiritual, a form of meditation on your partner, on the miracle of life and the miracle of love.

Our culture has very little understanding of sexuality and its true role, and we are suffering because of it.

America's moral roots lie in the Puritanism of those who originally settled this continent, and thus *we live in a society that has separated sexuality from life, disconnected it from the heart, and polluted it with guilt.* Sex is the most basic instinct we have as human beings, and yet many of us learn about it only through awkward and often painful experience. To make matters worse, we are brought up not to talk about it, and find it difficult to be sexually honest even with our husbands or wives, and often, with ourselves. For many Americans, sex is still in the closet.

The result is a population that is sexually unconscious, and when we're unconscious about something, we become repressed, obsessed, depressed, and dysfunctional. Rather than a source of joy, sex becomes a source of shame and frustration, or a weapon with which to punish our mate, or an addiction we use to numb ourselves to pain, or perhaps a substitute for love. **And when we are sexually unconscious, we can't experience real moments in our lovemaking.**

Some of the most powerful and significant moments you and your lover can share will happen when you introduce real moments into your sexual relationship, moments in which you aren't *trying* to achieve anything, or get it over with, moments when you are mindfully in the present, celebrating the body, heart, and soul of your beloved. Later in this book, I'll offer you some techniques for kissing, touching, and uniting that will help you reinvent your sexuality so you can use your sexual play not as an end in itself but as a starting point for a deepening of your love and intimacy. Then you will really be *making* love.

Using Real Moments to Make Love All the Time

Ultimately, *being a lover means not waiting until you have sex to make love with your partner.*

$\mathcal{M}$aking love is not just
about sex.
It is about making real moments of love
with your beloved.

If you limit your lovemaking to your sexual time together, you will put tremendous pressure on your sex life. You will be so hungry for love, for a true soul connection with your partner, that the sex will not be completely satisfying, no matter how good it is. That's because *it is not pleasure you're craving—it's real moments.*

I believe that the endless craving and obsession we have for sex in our society is really a craving for love. **Many people think they need more sex, but what they really need is more real moments.** If you long for real moments with your mate, it doesn't matter how many orgasms you have, or how many times a week you have sex. Your heart will still be hungry for love and connection.

It will help to stop thinking that lovemaking begins in the bedroom. *The bedroom may be a comfortable place to have sex, but if you wait until you get there to begin making love, you'll be too late, and your hearts and spirits may not have enough time to catch up to your bodies.* Then you will be left with what so many of us accept as a substitute for complete sexual union—if you're lucky, you will have good sex, but you will miss the ecstasy that can only occur when your body, your heart, and your spirit make love to those of your beloved all at the same time.

◆

So when does the lovemaking between two lovers start? It begins whenever you choose to have a real moment with your partner—just one moment when you allow yourself to fully feel your love for your mate, one moment when you surrender to the wonder of your relationship, one smile, one embrace, one gaze that says "I rejoice in the miracle that is us. . . ."

Be a husband or wife, a best friend, a coparent, and all else that makes up a full partnership. But remember to be a lover, at least for a little while each day. Look for opportunities to *make* love, to stir up the river of feeling that already flows between you. Find the love in your heart, and then be *in* love. Real moment upon real moment, you will always be making love together, and your joy will be unending.

2

The Courage to Love Deeply

*I*t doesn't take much courage to simply have a relationship. You choose to spend your time with someone, to have sex with him or her, perhaps to live in the same house. But it does take courage to love your partner deeply, to not be merely a couple but to be true lovers, and to walk the path of conscious relationship together.

Great love always requires great courage. It asks you to push past the fear that would keep you protected and invulnerable to your partner, and instead, to reveal your most secret hiding places and most unguarded doorways. It demands that you invite your beloved in and allow him to know all of you, the strength and the despair, the vision and the terror, the confident adult and the lonely child. It insists on showing you every place in your being that is selfish and strong willed, every shadow in your heart that is not loving or compassionate, so you see all the ways you need to grow as a lover.

> $\mathcal{G}$reat love will probably make you uncomfortable as it forces you to look into the mirror at yourself.

If you measure the success of your relationship in terms of how comfortable it makes you feel, you may delude yourself into believing that your stagnant relationship is good because it doesn't challenge you, and confuse yourself by thinking that your transforming relationship is unhealthy because it's pushing all of your buttons. I'm certainly *not* saying that a relationship that is *always* painful and unfulfilling is good for you, and you should remain with that partner—you shouldn't. **But when you have the courage to love deeply and consciously, you may find yourself uncomfortable much of the time, as your relationship stretches you beyond the boundaries of your ego and purifies both of you of all that is not loving about yourselves.**

> $\mathcal{W}$hen you love deeply, courageously and with commitment, you invite Truth into your relationship.

How many times, during an argument with your lover, have you listened to him or her complaining to you about what's wrong with the way you're loving or communicating in the relationship, and you found yourself thinking *"Hey, I don't need this!"*? My response is that *you do need it,* or it wouldn't be happening. I know—it seems ironic at times:

The more deeply and honestly you love, and the more trust you create between you, the more your partner and your relationship will confront you with the truth, and the more uncomfortable you may become!

This explains why couples often experience the period of time immediately following a deepening of their commitment, such as moving in together or getting married, as a time of increased tension and disagreement. The power of their vows and their intention to grow closer acts like a fire that "heats" up the temperature of the relationship until it reaches a boiling point when all the impurities rise to the surface. All of a sudden, you become aware of everything that is not loving about your partner and about yourself.

When you don't understand this principle, you can misinterpret something healthy and purifying that's happening in your relationship, and mistake it for something unhealthy and undesirable. You panic and think "Oh my gosh, things are falling apart between us," when actually, **things are trying to come more together.** It is at these times, then, when you need to find the courage to stay instead of running, the courage to move into the truth instead of away from it, the courage to remain open instead of closing off—*the courage to keep loving.*

The Courage to Share Real Moments

If loving deeply requires a certain degree of emotional courage, then sharing real moments with your beloved requires even more courage. Why? **Because real moments force you to feel what is** . . .

> *T*he more real moments you and
> your partner share together,
> the more difficult it will be for you to
> avoid
> the reality of your relationship.

The more honest, open moments you and your partner spend connecting from the heart, the harder it will be to pretend things are fine when they're not, to convince yourself that you're being loved enough when you aren't, and to ignore the shadows in your relationship. This is one of the main reasons many of us go to great lengths to avoid real moments—*they are confrontational; they force you out of your comfort zone; they demand that you pay attention.*

And so you don't seem to find the time for the difficult conversation with your mate that you've been meaning to have, or the quiet evening alone you've been promising yourselves, or the long, unrushed lovemaking session you both agree you need. *Something* always seems to get in the way. I don't care how logical your excuses *appear* to be — **you're avoiding these real moments because you're afraid of the feelings they might force you to face.**

◆

The courage to love deeply and share real moments is the courage to be naked with your lover, not just physically but emotionally. Physical nakedness is actually a lot less intimidating than emotional nakedness. When your clothes are off, all your partner sees is your body, but when your emotional walls are down, he can see much more — how much you need him, or how insecure you sometimes feel, or how angry you are even though you've been denying it, or how scared you are to really let go in bed.

Very few lovers spend enough time being really naked together:

> *B*eing naked isn't about
> taking off your clothes —
> it's about taking off your mask
> and revealing the feelings at the core
> of who you are.

Have you ever looked at your mate and known there was a whole world of feeling inside of him that he wasn't showing you? Have you ever asked your lover "What's wrong?" because you knew she was unhappy, only to have her coldly respond: "Nothing"? Or has *your* lover ever reached out to you with an open heart, and you've found *yourself* unwilling to open up and let him in? These are some of the ways we keep our "emotional clothes" on, that we avoid real moments of nakedness.

When you and your lover are physically naked, skin against skin, you experience an intimacy, an innocence, and a vulnerability that is hard to create when you are fully clothed. *So too, when you both find the courage to be emotionally naked, soul touching soul, you will discover each other in a way you cannot without these real moments of self-disclosure.*

If you have a lover, and you trust him, take off your clothes—the ones you wear on the outside, and the ones you use to cover yourself on the inside. **Get naked together, in every way possible, and as often as possible.**

Loving Begins With You

One of the greatest misconceptions we have about love is that it is some force outside of ourselves that will magically descend upon us and fill us with passion and feeling. It may seem this way when you first fall in love, as if your heart has been suddenly opened by your lover, and into it, he or she has poured all sorts of delicious emotions. For a while, your relationship feeds off that initial high. Eventually, however, the love doesn't feel as sharp and strong as it did in the beginning, and so *you wait for your lover to do something to make you feel more in love with him.*

Waiting for your partner to fill you up with love is a mistake. **You need to learn how to continually fall in love with him or her over and over again.**

*L*ove always starts with you.
It is a choice that you make,
from moment to moment,
to look for what is lovable about your
partner.

When you wait for the person you love to do or say something that will **make you** feel more in love, you're setting him up to inevitably disappoint you. *It is not his job to be lovable. It is your job to be loving to him*—to know his needs and attempt to satisfy them, to give him attention, affection, and appreciation, to let him know, through your kindness, your consideration, and your words, that you value the gift of his presence in your life. And likewise, it is his job to be loving to you, and do all these same things. This kind of giving needs lots of real moments when you leave yourself and your ego behind, and choose to move your awareness into your lover's world, your lover's mind, your lover's heart. You feel him fully, from the inside out, asking yourself what he wants and needs from you. Every day, you ask your-self the question:

"How can I love him or her more?"

Hopefully, your partner is asking himself the same ques-tion and longing to please you as much as you long to please him. Even if he's not at first, when you choose moments in which you're loving this way, you will find that you end up feeling more *in* love with your beloved.

This is *not* about becoming a self-sacrificing, totally powerless person who neglects yourself and your own needs in order to make someone else happy. **In fact, if you aren't good at loving yourself, you will have a difficult time loving anyone, since you'll resent the time and energy you give them that you aren't even giving to yourself.** Loving, like all else in life, must be performed in a balanced way. You *must* know and fulfill your own needs, and be sure that loving your mate never compromises your personal values or integrity. And you also must be with a partner who is committed to working on himself and the relationship as intently as you are, so you aren't the only one giving.

I call this practice *"Choosing to Love,"* because the courage to love deeply means making the choice to love over and over again. **When you <u>both</u> stop waiting for your partner to start loving you until you love, and just *choose* to love the other first, your relationship will begin to feel full and flowing.**

✦

This is how it should go, then, the dance of love. You discover the courage to take the first step, and your partner discovers the courage to take the first step, and all of a sudden you find yourselves *stepping into love together,* moving to your own intimate rhythm, surrendering to the Oneness that awaits you.

3

Using Your Relationship as a Sanctuary

Of all the places you can go in the world, none should feel safer than your intimate relationship. The emotional and physical home you and your partner create should, at its best, be a haven, *a shelter of positive energy* that can offer you courage and clarity, comfort and support whenever life challenges you with difficulties. You may not always choose to use your relationship this way—sometimes you will need to find solace and answers from within yourself—but in your heart, you will always know the relationship is there, a light shining in the dark that will always guide you back to where you belong.

This is not the way it is for many lovers. Instead of seeing your relationship as a refuge that will restore your strength and calm your spirit, perhaps you view it as just *one more part of your life that will drain and deplete you.* Instead of looking forward to being with your partner, knowing that connecting with him or her will replenish and energize you, *you avoid the person you love the most, fearing that being together will only further sap your energy.* And so you withdraw into yourself, and disconnect from your beloved.

◆

When relationships are at their worst, you not only can't imagine turning to your lover for emotional nourishment—**you feel your lover himself is the source of your pain and turmoil.** This only fuels your desire to pull away, emotionally and physically. And sometimes, it's true—if you are with the **wrong** person, or if your partner hasn't fully committed to you and the relationship, or if he or she has old, unresolved emotional patterns that prevent him from giving you the love you want, you may need to pull back in order to find your center, or to gather the strength to give an ultimatum, or to find the courage to leave.

Of course, there will be times in even the best relationships when you don't feel safe, when you need other people's perspective and support, when you and your partner are in a process of tension and disagreement. **But it should not feel that way all the time, or even most of the time:**

Something is wrong with a relationship when you don't feel safe reaching out to your partner for comfort. . . .

Something is wrong with a relationship when you trust other people with your pain more than you do your own mate. . . .

Something is wrong with a relationship when you cannot turn to it and find the peace you've been seeking. . . .

Your relationship should be a place you often retreat to, not a place you run from.

You deserve to feel that you can turn to your lover to be your emotional sanctuary, and your lover deserves to feel he can turn to you for the same. *In order for this to happen, you need to be comfortable sharing real moments together.* After all, it's never mere words or gestures that make you feel protected and nourished by your partner—it's the feeling you get when he holds you tightly in his arms, or when she wraps her warm body around yours as if to say "Everything will be all right," or the look he gives you as you pour your heart out, a look that promises he'll never go away. **It is the very timelessness and simplicity of those intimate real moments that will create the peace and safety you are looking for.**

◆

The first step is learning to recognize the signs that your lover is in need of a sanctuary. Can you tell

when she needs a hug? Are you aware of how he be-
haves when he is feeling frightened? Do you know when
she needs to talk about something? Most people won't
come out and say "I'm in emotional overwhelm right
now, and I need you to be my sanctuary," so until you
and your partner learn to ask for that kind of nurturing,
you each should be on the lookout for the often silent
cries for help the other gives you. If you aren't sure what
they are, ask your mate: *"How do you usually behave
when you're upset and need extra love and support
from me?"*

Once you become familiar with the signs that your
lover could use some real moments, **you need to learn
to become a *sanctuary* for him or her.** This is often a
lot more challenging than it sounds. You may feel that
you make it safe for your lover to open up to you and
reach out for comfort, but in actuality, you may be making it harder than it needs to be. Something that I've had
a difficult time accepting and am still working hard to
put into practice is the understanding *that being an emotional refuge for your lover does not mean fixing him or
solving the problem.* **It's not about *doing* anything—it's
about just *being there* in a real moment of your love
for him.**

*Do you know how to love your lover through his distress
or pain without trying to fix him? Do you know how to give
comfort and support, even if it doesn't seem like it's helping
or making a difference? Do you know how to be there for*

your partner in the way <u>he</u> wants you to be there, rather than in the way <u>you</u> enjoy being there?

These aren't easy emotional tasks to accomplish, especially if you are normally an achiever and like to see instant results from whatever you focus your efforts on. It will help to remind yourself to be fully in the moment with your mate, not expecting anything, not trying to achieve a particular outcome, but simply loving him or her with all of your being.

If you're not sure that you are a good *"love sanctuary,"* ask your partner what he thinks. Be willing to receive feedback about how he would like you to be there for him, and what he needs to experience real moments of comfort and healing. This is one of the greatest gifts you can give the person you love—the knowledge that you will be there, waiting to love him, when he needs it the most.

> *W*hen your relationship is filled
> with real moments,
> it will cease to feel like
> an obligation or burden
> and, instead, become a healing
> sanctuary.

If you don't seek sanctuary in your relationship, you will end up seeking it somewhere else. It's that simple. You cannot deny the human need you have to be soothed, to be sheltered, to ease the pain. **So if you do not or cannot turn to your beloved, you will turn to whatever else you are substituting for love—food, drugs, or alcohol, addictive sex, incessant work—anything that temporarily numbs or distracts you.**

The problem with all addictions is that they are substitutes for the real thing, and therefore will not satisfy the hunger for the compassion and tenderness your spirit really craves. Yes, sometimes it seems so much less complicated to pour yourself a drink than to turn to your husband and say "I'm hurting, and I need you to hold me." Sometimes it seems much less confrontational to work until midnight than to say to your wife "I'm frightened that business is so bad right now, and I need to know you're still proud of me, and love me anyway." *Real moments aren't always easy moments. But they will nourish you in ways only real moments can.*

◆

My husband and I have a very special sculpture in our house of two big bears sitting back to back, leaning against one another as they both gaze upward with contented looks on their faces. The first time we saw this piece of art, we knew it was made for us—it reflects much of what I've talked about in this chapter. I wrote this poem to honor the visual reminder the bears gave us of **how to use your beloved for strength and support without losing yourself in the process.**

THE BEARS

These bears have come into our lives
      to teach us about love.
If we look at them closely, we will learn everything
      we need to learn to be happy:

See how content and peaceful the bears look?
That's because they are leaning
      against one another.
Back to back they sit,
      supported by each other's strength,
      comforted by the other's presence,
Yet still free to look off in their own direction,
      dreaming their own dreams,
      gazing at their own horizons,
And all the while, knowing their companion is near.

Their posture calls for a complete commitment
      to one another,
Yet that commitment only allows each of them
      to do what, alone, they could not comfortably do.

When I see these bears, I see the truth
      about what love and commitment really mean.
When I see these bears, I see the true essence of
      our relationship.

Lean against me, my beloved,
      as I lean on you.

I will be your strength and your comfort.
I will support you, with love and friendship,
    as you gaze off in your own special direction,
    dreaming your own dreams.

Lean against me and feel how our love
    only strengthens your own freedom
    to be the best you can be.

Know that I am here,
    always behind you,
    your lover, your companion,
    your family, your soul's true friend.

◆

I share this very special poem with you who are lovers like myself, as a reminder to us all to cherish the refuge of our love. Use your relationship as the safe and healing sanctuary it was meant to be. Lean on your beloved, and be there so he can lean on you.

Part Two

◆

REAL
MOMENTS
AND
EVERYDAY
INTIMACY

4

The Loving Gaze

$\mathcal{T}$he eyes of your beloved are the windows through which you can gaze into his or her soul. When you look deeply into the eyes of the one you love, you will see beyond his face, beyond the physical form, and glimpse the essence of who he is. You will learn things about your lover that you cannot learn from words. You will feel the truth.

Most of us are not very good at looking directly into a person's eyes, or allowing them to look into ours. We live in a world where we avoid making eye contact, even with the people we love the most. We find it difficult to hold someone's gaze for more than a few seconds without becoming extremely uncomfortable. It feels too personal, too intrusive, as if our boundaries are being violated.

What is it that frightens us when someone looks into our eyes? Perhaps we feel they will see parts of us that we'd prefer to keep hidden—our insecurities, our anger, our neediness. Perhaps we're afraid they will penetrate through our protections and get too close. So we avert our gaze, make idle conversation, laugh at nothing, find an excuse to look at something else, anything to escape their eyes.

Often, it is just as scary for *you* to really look into the eyes of someone you love as it is for him to look at you, for when you do, you may see everything you've been hoping to avoid—your lover's indifference, or his wounds still fresh from something hurtful that you said or did, or his deep love that you're not sure you can return.

You and your lover can feel more naked, more vulnerable, when you share a loving gaze together than when you take off your clothes. This is why truly connecting with your eyes and gazing at one another is one of the best ways to deepen your bond and create real moments.

Some of the most profound real moments you and your lover can share will happen when you begin to really look into each other's eyes.

Looking <u>into</u> someone's eyes is not the same as looking <u>at</u> him. When you look <u>at</u> someone, **your intention is to stay separate from that person, to view him while your awareness remains in your own space.** That is what makes him so uncomfortable—you are seeing him, but he cannot *feel* you there with him. The distance between you is what might give him the sensation that he is being judged or analyzed.

Looking <u>into</u> your lover's eyes, your intention is that the boundaries between you will temporarily dissolve, and for a moment, your souls will touch. You are looking into him, and opening yourself so he can look into you at the same time. It's as if your eyes are connected to your heart, allowing it to "see" your beloved. **This is what I call the "loving gaze."**

◆

One of the most basic needs we have as human beings is to be visible, to be seen, to know our existence has been acknowledged by others. This is why it hurts someone you love when you ignore him more than it does when you express anger toward him. Making someone feel invisible is like saying *"You don't count, you make no difference to me or to my life."*

Too often in our intimate relationships we feel that who we really are is not being acknowledged and seen by our partner. He sleeps next to you, makes love to you, eats breakfast and dinner with you, sometimes looks *at* you but doesn't really look *into* you. He sees your face, but doesn't see your feelings. He sees your body, but doesn't see your spirit.

This is "soul loneliness"—the emptiness you feel when the person you love doesn't truly *see* you. You are together, but you feel as if you are alone. You live with a secret longing, the dream that your beloved could see your soul, that his gaze would penetrate through the layers of your being into the depths of who you are, and that in spite of everything he saw, he would love you anyway.

*W*hen your partner looks at you with a
loving gaze,
you will feel more completely loved
than if he gave you any gift,
more perfectly beautiful than if
he said any words,
for the silence creates a sacred space
in which you can receive his love
in its purest form.

Does your wife seem hungry for your love and attention? Maybe she needs you to take her hands and look with a loving gaze into her being for a few moments, until she can feel that, yes, even though you've been distracted lately, your love for her is intact. Do you suspect that your husband feels you give too much attention to running your household and raising your children, and there is none left for him? Hold his face in your hands, and look with a loving gaze into his heart, until he can feel your love pouring into his being.

Learning to Share a Loving Gaze

Here is a guide to help you to practice the *loving gaze* with your partner. You can take turns doing this to one another, or for best results, you can both practice the loving gaze at the same time. Even if you don't think your partner will try this, you can practice the loving gaze by yourself and still have a wonderful experience.

◆

To begin, make sure you're in a place where you won't be interrupted or distracted, especially when you're just learning. Once you become good at the loving gaze, you'll be able to practice it anywhere.

Sit comfortably. If you'd like, take your partner's hands. Focus your awareness gently on your partner's eyes. Don't stare—*just allow your eyes to relax as they make contact with his eyes.* Be sure to take some deep breaths. Now, imagine that you're looking **into** his eyes, traveling past them. Don't get stuck on the physical appearance of the eyes—look beyond them.

Look for the vulnerable little child that your partner still is. . . .
Look for the dreamer in him that wants so much. . . .

Look for the goodness in his spirit. . . .
Now, look even deeper, and look for the love. . . .
Feel your mate as a pure expression of love.

Send him the silent message:

> **"I see who you really are,
> and I love you."**

Then, **imagine a channel inside your body connecting your heart with your eyes, and visualize all the love you feel for your partner pouring up from your heart, pouring out through your eyes, flowing into the eyes of your partner and down into his heart.**
Imagine *flooding him with love through your eyes,* healing every wounded place, filling up every empty space inside of him.

Feel your love blessing him.
Feel the act of loving him blessing you.

If your partner is "love gazing" with you, notice how the boundaries between you are dissolving, so that you can't feel where you stop and he begins—*all you can feel is the flow of love between you.*

Breathe into that love, and soon you'll become aware that your partner has disappeared, and you have disappeared, and all that remains is love. . . .

✦

It takes practice to become good at love gazing. At first, you may feel nervous or awkward. You might even notice that you or your partner has some resistance to surrendering to the process and allowing yourself to experience real moments looking *into* each other. **The more you relax and feel yourself right there, totally in the moment, the easier it will be to see into the window of your lover's eyes, and allow him to see into yours, so together, you can discover the sweetness that is your love.**

Looking for the Beauty in Your Lover

The *loving gaze* is a wonderful technique for experiencing real moments with the person you love. But even the way you use your vision in everyday situations can enhance or detract from your relationship. Learning to see your lover differently can add new dimensions of closeness and attraction to your relationship. I call this *"looking for the beauty in your lover."*

The human form is an amazing work of art. From the top of our heads to the tip of our toes, there is so much about us that is beautiful. When you first fall in love, you are fully aware of your partner's beauty—everything about him or her seems perfect. Then, as time passes, and you become accustomed to looking at your mate each day, *you forget to look at him with eyes of love.* In-

stead, you begin to see all the things that aren't perfect—the growing bald spot, the extra fat around the
middle, the features that are out of proportion.

All of us are far from physically perfect. If your eyes
look for imperfection in your mate, they will find it.

> ## *W*hen you focus on your partner's
> lack of beauty,
> your eyes become the enemy of your
> loving relationship.

We live in a society obsessed with physical appearance and unmindful of spiritual beauty, and the result is
that far too often, we put our attention on what is not
physically right about our partner instead of what *is*
beautiful about him, inside and out. *The more you notice
what isn't perfect about your mate, the more turned off you
become, until you've destroyed all sexual chemistry between you.*

Your eyes don't merely see—they give off energy.
Have you ever had someone give you a look that made
you tingle all over with pleasure, or made you feel as if
you'd been stabbed with daggers, or filled you up with
strength and courage? Their eyes didn't just passively
see you . . . they passed an energy to you, an energy you
took in through your eyes.

In this same way, how you use your eyes in your relationship can have a positive or negative effect on your
partner. Each glance you send his or her way can create

more love, or more mistrust and distance, between you. You won't have to say anything—he will feel loved or not loved by the way you look at him. **Your eyes cannot lie.**

✦

Start loving your partner with your eyes. Learn to consciously and actively *look for* the beautiful, the graceful, the miraculous in the physical package your soul mate has arrived in—the delicate way she moves her hands; the strong curve in his back; the silky texture of her hair; the solidity of his body. Use the energy from your eyes to adore and caress him, to search out and appreciate all the everyday wonders he possesses, so that each time you look at your lover, you find more reasons to fall deeper in love.

5

Loving Your Partner With Words

*B*ecoming a good lover means becoming good at connecting. *Love thrives on connection.* It cannot exist without it, for it is *the connection between you and the person you love that allows for the flow of love, and that creates the experience of intimacy.*

Many lovers connect primarily through sex, using their bodies as the link that builds the experience of intimacy. So when sex is good and frequent, they feel happy and in love. When sex is not fulfilling or infrequent, they feel distant and detached. And often, when they feel the desire to connect and be close to their mate, they find themselves craving sex, for it's the only way they know how to find moments of oneness.

Sex is a wonderful way to connect with the person

you love, but it is just one of many. *Learning to experience more real moments with your partner requires learning to connect deeply and intimately in as many ways as possible.*

> *T*he more connections you
> and your lover make,
> not just between your bodies,
> but between your minds, your hearts,
> and your souls,
> the more you will strengthen
> the fabric of your relationship,
> and the more real moments you will
> experience together.

One of the best ways to create intimate connections between you and your beloved is with **words.** *Words are* bridges *that allow you to travel from your private world into your partner's.* They link your silences together, so you can know the person you love from the inside out, and he can know you. They banish the illusion that no one can ever understand you. They remind you that you are not alone.

Words are verbal souvenirs of the invisible dance you and your loved one are engaged in. They give your mind evidence to trust what your heart already knows. Deep inside, you *feel* he loves you, but when you hear him say those words, the experience becomes that much more real.

Words are necessary because they take the formless energy that love is and wrap it into packages. *They furnish your feelings with concrete form so they can be passed on to your mate.* Each expression of caring, of appreciation, of gratitude becomes a beautiful present you offer your beloved.

Some people argue that words, by definition, cannot possibly contain the fullness of emotion, and therefore limit your experience of intimacy. "Talking about it trivializes the love," they insist. I strongly disagree— **without words to make the feelings tangible and transferable, the feelings will not be as real to you or to your partner.**

Words stir up the love energy between you. They are like the wind, making waves upon the ocean of feeling you share. The water is always there in the sea, but it is the wind that moves it, teasing it from stillness until it rises into sparkling swells. Your feelings are always there in your heart, but it is the words that give them movement from silence into expression.

*W*ords help love dance and celebrate itself.

Many lovers are stingy with their words. They hoard them as if they have a limited number of *"I love you's,"* *"I need you's,"* and *"You make me so happy's"* available and don't want to use them up. So they conserve the amount of verbal love they share, saving it for special occasions such as birthdays or anniversaries, and leave their partner feeling hungry for words the majority of the time.

Whenever I've confronted verbally stingy men in my life, they always responded with this defensive reasoning for why they weren't loving me more with words:

"If I say it all the time, it won't mean anything anymore. . . ."

This thinking is as absurd as believing that if you wear a beautiful dress often, it won't be as beautiful as if you wear it only once in a while, or that if you kiss your little girl or boy good night *every night* and tell them you love them, it won't mean as much as if you do it only once every four months! *The result of this kind of emotional stinginess will be that your partner feels controlled and resentful.*

Words lose their meaning only when there is no genuine feeling behind them. If I don't really feel that I love you, but I tell you I do, those words are meaningless *not* because of how often I say them, but because they are not coming from my heart. Repetition does not "wear out" the significance behind the words—they will be as significant as the degree to which you are in the moment when you express them.

> *L*ove isn't like fat or cholesterol—
> there is no need to limit our
> consumption of it, no sense in
> assuming that less love is better
> than more love.

Have you ever been putting your lover on a *"verbal love diet"* without realizing it? Are you doling out little tastes of love that leave your lover hungry and always wanting more? Or perhaps it's your lover who's been starving <u>you</u> by controlling the amount of love words he gives you.

Most of us need to learn to use *more* words of love, and not *fewer* words. And most of us need more verbal love from our partners. **Words of love will feed your partner's heart and nourish his spirit.** How many more of our relationships would survive and flourish if only we were more generous with our words!!

$\mathcal{S}$haring words of love
is one of the simplest ways for lovers
to create instant real moments.

Words About Yourself

Words that you speak about yourself open the door to your spirit so that your partner can enter and see the fullness and uniqueness that is you. They invite your lover into your inner sanctuary of dreams and desires, feelings and fantasies. *How else is he to know the vast territory of your inner reality unless you offer him a map?* How else will he learn what hurts you, what delights you, and what makes you feel loved?

*L*oving your partner means using words to help him know you and love you better.

One of the most certain ways to sabotage your relationship is to believe the romantic myth that says: *"If my partner is the right one for me, if he really loves me, he will automatically know just what I need."* So you sit back and wait for him to prove himself, unconsciously testing him by *not* asking for what you want emotionally or sexually.

When you don't use words to give your lover a road map into your being, you will wait for him in vain, for he will get lost trying to please you. "He's failed to love me the way I need to be loved," you conclude with bitterness. But the truth will be that *you set him up for certain failure, and set yourself up for disappointment and betrayal by not using words to show him the way to your heart.*

Translating your feelings into words isn't always easy. Some of us aren't very familiar with the language of love, because no one ever used it with us. *"I don't like talking about feelings—that's just the way I am,"* we claim. Some of us feel uncomfortable using words, either because we fear we aren't very good with them or because expressing our emotions in words leaves us feeling vulnerable and unprotected. *"I'm not sure what to say . . . I just can't describe it,"* or *"I don't want to talk about it,"* we protest.

Your fear or lack of ability is no
excuse for not learning how to use
words
to be a better lover.

Making Love With Words

Do you know how to make love to someone with words? Do you know how to talk to her body until it opens for you like a flower? Do you know how to tell him how much you want him until he swells with desire?

There is a time during sexual lovemaking for silence, and there is also a time for words. Words add a whole other dimension to lovemaking. They create yet another channel across which your love can flow. While the movement of your body and the sounds you make communicate to your partner's body, *words communicate your passion to your lover's brain.* And it's the brain that controls all the pleasure centers in your body.

The words you share
when you make love
turn on your brain
and help it turn on your body.

Words also have the power to open up your heart and the heart of your beloved. *They unlock whatever protec-*

tive walls you may have built around you, so that you feel more during sex, not just physically but emotionally. And it is the feeling that begins to transform sex into true love-making.

✦

Many people avoid using words during sex because words of desire make them feel too naked and exposed. I can be *feeling* that my lover's touch makes me hot, but if I say to him "Your touch makes me so hot," now I am sure that *he knows,* and now I am more vulnerable. My words give him power over me, the power that comes from knowing his seduction has been successful, from knowing that I want him.

If you have any feelings of guilt or shame about your sexuality that you've taken on from your upbringing, your religious background, or any past traumatic sexual experiences, you will probably avoid using words during lovemaking, and even have a difficult time hearing them from your lover. **Words make what you're doing real.** It's as if you've made a secret agreement with yourself: "I can have sex as long as I don't *say* I'm having sex. I can feel pleasure as long as I don't *admit* that I'm feeling pleasure."

If sex is frightening or uncomfortable for you, ask your partner to use words to help you heal those feelings. He can gently whisper, *"You're safe . . . I'll never hurt you . . . I love you for who you are on the inside . . . It's okay to let go and enjoy our love . . ."* or whatever phrases you think will combat any negative mental programming you have, and remind you that physically loving your partner is a natural, sacred experience you deserve to have.

◆

You have the power to make your lover smile with delight. You have the power to make her weep with happiness. You have the power to make him feel so safe, so understood, that all his old fear and mistrust just melt away. You have the power to make her feel so cherished, so beautiful, that never again will she feel jealous or insecure.

This power is in your words. Your words of love are the priceless treasures whose value can never be measured. You can use them to fill your lover's heart and caress his spirit. You can use them to create an unbreakable bond between you. And most of all, you can use them to create joy, right here, right now. *For each time you share words of love, you will be giving yourselves the gift of a real moment . . .*

6

The Timeless Embrace

*W*hen words aren't needed, or when words aren't enough, or when there are no words left, then it is time to just hold the person you love in your arms. Hold him when he's frightened, or in pain, and there's nothing else you can do. Hold her when she looks so beautiful that she takes your breath away. Hold him when you see him struggling to find his feelings. Hold her when you both know you've been taking her for granted.

There is a power in a simple embrace that can be more intimate than the most passionate sex, and more meaningful than the most honest conversation. When someone holds you, and you allow yourself to surrender to the love he surrounds you with, you enter a sacred place. The world around you fades away, and your universe is contained in the space within his arms. Time seems to stop. Nothing else exists, nothing else matters.

*W*ithin the sacred circle
of your lover's arms,
you can find healing, wholeness,
and redemption.

*W*ithin the safety
of your lover's embrace,
you can come back to *now*,
and experience a real moment.

A true embrace will almost automatically produce a real moment, because it forces you into the *now*. When you and your lover hold one another, you aren't actively *doing* anything. You're not trying to turn each other on, or trying to give advice, or trying to get your partner to talk about the relationship, or trying to do any of the other things lovers do to and with one another—you're just *being* together.

Whenever you need to return to the essence of your love, ask your partner to hold you. Something magical can happen to you when you are held in your lover's arms. You forget about things that you thought mattered, and remember the things that really do matter. You get out of your head and back into your heart. You stop feeling like strangers or enemies and recall your oneness. Sharing that moment of *timeless together-ness,* you are able to rediscover your loving connection.

✦

Some of us mistake everyday hugs for true em-braces. There's a big difference between a *hug* and an *embrace.* When you give or receive a hug, you hold the other person for just a moment, often rushing to termi-nate the connection so it doesn't become too intimate. When you and your lover embrace, your intention is just the opposite—*you want to linger in the experience for as long as possible, to use the moment to intensify the inti-macy between you.*

$\mathcal{L}$overs often use hugs to avoid embracing, communicating, or really feeling each other.

You substitute a quick hug for what your partner really needs—for you to share how much you appreciate her, for you to apologize for ignoring him lately, for you to say "I miss you, and I want to connect with you again." Hugs are wonderful, but not as a replacement for a true loving embrace.

The Healing Power of a True Embrace

Your first experience of love was most likely a joyous embrace by your mother moments after you were born.

Curled up in her arms, breathing your first breaths, you felt welcomed, protected, safe. Her energy enveloped you and created a womblike sanctuary into which you eagerly retreated.

This is why being held is such a basic and primal experience. It takes you back to your very beginnings. It reminds you, once again, how to just surrender and allow yourself to be taken care of. It teaches you how to receive.

*W*hen you are embraced with love, the child within you can emerge.

There, in your lover's arms, you may find yourself feeling small and vulnerable, just as you did when you were young. Your head lies against his shoulder, you hold him tightly and close your eyes. Named and unnamed fears and demons begin to float into your awareness, some left over from childhood, some fresh from recent challenges or disappointments. Neither of you says anything, but *slowly, you feel a new sense of peace spreading through your being, as the silent love you're sharing soothes your spirit and mends your heart.*

◆

Last night I burned my fingers trying to fix some electrical equipment that was very hot. I walked into the room where my husband was watching television and showed him the injury. The first thing he did was to get some ice for my hand. And the second thing he did was to hold me. With one arm around my shoulders and one stroking my hair, he sat with me for several minutes.

As I leaned against my husband's body, I allowed myself to totally sink into the moment: . . . I was a small child of three who had just badly scraped her knee, but never got to be held by Daddy because he didn't come home that night.

. . . I was a little girl of ten who fell off her bicycle and felt humiliated that I wasn't as athletic as the other kids.

. . . I was a woman of twenty and twenty-five and thirty who had felt so lonely in my relationships and longed for the man I loved to hold me, just like this.

. . . And I was me, right now, grown up and able to take care of myself, but smart enough to know that an embrace still makes anything hurt less, and so grateful that I had finally found someone to hold me with love.

◆

Here's how to use these real moments together to allow your old pain to be healed:

When you are being embraced by your lover, breathe in the love you are receiving, and as you exhale, visualize the loving energy surrounding a piece of your past you'd like healed.

Imagine that your lover is holding all the wounded parts of you at different ages. Feel each person you used to be when you were hurt, whether you were a small child or an adult, and visualize your partner

actually embracing that person. *If you are both willing, you can even ask your partner to say certain phrases to those wounded parts of you that will help your healing process, such as "You're perfect just the way you are," "You don't have to work hard to get me to love you," "You're safe with me and my love will protect you," etc.*

Notice any resistance you have to being loved, and just breathe through it. Allow yourself to drink in the love you're receiving, until you feel the old pain subside, and in its place, a sense of contentment, completion, and peace.

◆

Here's how to hold your partner in a healing embrace:

As you put your arms around your lover, close your eyes and allow yourself to feel the places inside of him that have been hurt or unloved. You might visualize those places as an emptiness that needs to be filled or a fire that needs to be extinguished. As you breathe in, feel yourself fill up with your love for your partner, and as you exhale, imagine that love pouring into him, soothing the old pain, replenishing his heart.

Now, visualize the wounded parts of your lover as if they are actually right there in your arms — *the frightened little boy, the young man who was betrayed, the husband who sometimes feels like a failure — and feel yourself loving each of them. If you wish, you can talk to those pieces of your lover out loud, using phrases such as the ones* *in the previous exercise. You can also just think these phrases silently to yourself.*

I encourage you and your partner to try sharing the healing embrace together. It will offer you some of your most precious real moments. If you think your mate might not be interested in this kind of intimacy, you can practice your part of the healing embrace anytime you hold him, and he doesn't even have to know about it. You may be surprised to find him suddenly opening up to you, or feeling better, without quite understanding why!

◆

Today, tonight, embrace the person you love. Don't explain yourself, just reach out and take him or her in your arms. Enter fully into the moment, and think to yourself:

"In my arms, I am holding all that is dear to me. I am holding my friend, my playmate, my beloved. I am holding a gift from God.

"I am blessed."

Part Three

◆

REAL MOMENTS
AND
SEXUAL LOVE

7

The Power of Loving Touch

*W*hen you and your lover are ready to enter into the dance of sexual loving together, when it is time to leave the separate worlds of your two bodies and join them as one, your reunion will begin with touch. Deep within you, a longing stirs—to feel the form of your beloved beneath your fingers, to feel the heat of his flesh next to yours, as if to reassure yourself that he is real, that your love is real. You may not even have the conscious thought, "I need to touch him," but your heart has spoken, and your body will listen.

From within the boundaries of your physical universe, your hand reaches out and travels across the space that separates you and your lover, the space that defines you as two, until suddenly, your hand makes contact with its destination—an arm, a thigh, a face, another hand, and *instantly, everything is different.* You are touching the outer edges of your partner's world. You can feel him in there, all of him, beyond the door-way of his skin. You will never get to physically touch the totality of the formless being housed inside, but for now, this is enough. The connection has been made, and its solidity reassures you that you are not alone.

✦

When we think of touch as just a physical or sexual act, we are cheating ourselves and our lover, because touch can be and ultimately is so much more.

*J*ust as worlds build bridges
between your mind and the mind of
your lover,
it is touch that builds bridges
between your bodies,
and allows you to have
a physical experience of the invisible
energy you feel in your hearts,
the energy we call "love."

Touch is the language of love. It is a language with no sound, no rules, no form. Through your hands, your heart speaks to your beloved, expressing feelings in a way mere words cannot. The tender caress of her face, the sensual stroke down his back, the grazing of your fingers across her belly—these gestures transcend the limitations of spoken language and communicate your desire, your need, your emotions more powerfully and more poignantly than words ever could.

Teaching Your Hands the Language of Love

Being a good lover means training your hands to speak the language of love with grace and eloquence. Like any language, the language of touch must be learned, practiced, and mastered if you are to become fluent in it. Having hands and fingers doesn't automatically mean you will know how to use them to speak to your lover's heart, any more than having paint and a paintbrush would automatically make you an artist.

Many of us have never learned how to use touch in a conscious, loving way. Instead, we carelessly paw, poke, probe, grab, grope, yank, squeeze, and rub, like a two-year-old throwing pieces of words together, never worrying about whether or not what he's saying makes sense. If you've ever been touched like this, you may remember lying there in disbelief, thinking to yourself, "Does he (or she) actually think *this* feels *good*?" And if you have ever touched your partner in this thoughtless manner, well perhaps this accounts for your lover's apparent disinterest in sex, lack of response during the act, or sudden headaches that conveniently appear when he or she senses your hands making their way toward their unhappy target.

Sadly, most of the inadequate and accidental sex education we received as adolescents had to do with **where** to touch someone to turn them on. We memorized three or four "hot spots" and, during our sexual encounters, faithfully tried to hit each one for at least a few minutes.

> *I*t's not enough to know
> *where* to touch your partner . . . you have
> to know *how* to touch him or her.

Many lovers know all the right places to touch—they just aren't touching in the right way. (And by the way, if your partner doesn't even know *where* to touch, show him—he won't figure it out by himself . . .)

The Magical Power of Your Hands

To begin learning *how* to touch with love, you need to understand and appreciate the magic that is contained in your hands:

Your hands are not just physical appendages. They are transmitters of the powerful life energy that flows through your body. The Eastern system of medicine explains that there are hundreds of meridians, or energetic pathways that run like highways throughout your body. Life energy moves along these pathways, and according to this system, many of these energy meridians end in your fingertips. *That means your hands can give off tremendous amounts of energy.* This, then, is why touch is so powerful:

*W*hen you touch your partner,
your hands aren't simply
stimulating nerve endings that make
him or her feel pleasure;
they are actually sending life energy
into your lover's body.

All hands can be healing hands, not only those that belong to healers. This is why you feel better after receiving a massage, or why your child stops crying when you rub his back, or why when you are in pain, your own hand naturally goes to touch the place that hurts on your body. You may not understand *how* this principle works, but you're already experiencing it working every day of your life.

Try this experiment to see if you can feel the energy emanating from your hands:

*When you've finished reading this paragraph, put the book down for a moment, place your right hand in front of you, thumb on top and pinky on the bottom, as if you were going to shake hands with someone. Then, place your left hand very close to your right hand so that the two hands are parallel but **not quite touching.** Very slowly, move your* *hands toward one another so that they almost touch, and then very slowly, move them about a half inch apart. Do this several times. If you pay attention, you should notice a light sensation in your hands as they get closer to each other, as if something is touching them.* **What you're feeling is the energy radiating from your hands.**

Unfortunately, all of the energy we carry within our body isn't always loving and healing. Sometimes we are carrying angry energy, fearful energy, or some other form of inharmonious energy. *Old, unexpressed hurts or grievances, past or present resentments you haven't re-leased, tension you haven't resolved—all of these can "leak" through your hands when you touch someone.* These emotions don't even have to be about the person you love. They might have their source in a former partner, or in an emotional wound from your childhood. But when you open the door to your heart and let the love flow, they rush out too.

*W*hatever is in your heart will come out through your hands.

What comes through your hands when you touch the person you love will depend on the quality of emotional energy inside of you, and what comes through your partner's hands when he or she touches you will depend on what's inside of him or her.

This is the power of touch. Ultimately, how your partner feels when he or she is touched by you will depend on what's inside your heart. You can read every book on sex that there is, and learn exotic techniques for arousing your partner, *but if you're touching her mechanically from your head, and not also loving her from your heart, there won't be much life energy flowing from your hands, and all your efforts to turn your lover on will have little or no effect.*

You can lie with words, but not with your hands. Your hands don't know how to lie. Either they're transmitting love energy, or they're not. You cannot fake a loving touch, because *it's not what your hands are* doing *that makes your partner feel loved—*it's the love you are feeling inside that radiates from your hands.

Most women are more sensitive to this than most men, for it is more difficult for us to become aroused merely from physical stimulation. . . .

We need to feel the love in our partner's hands. . . .

We need to feel his emotional presence there with us. . . .

We need to be made love to, and not just turned on.

*I*t is the love behind the touch,
and not the touch itself,
that will make it safe enough
for a woman's erotic nature to unfold.

Turning Your Partner on With Love

Love is the greatest turn-on that there is. The energy that is love makes our cells vibrate with delight and makes our souls rejoice. When you allow your love to flow from your heart and into your hands, your partner will feel as if your hands are charged with electricity, and every caress will be pleasurable beyond anything he or she has ever experienced before.

If you want to become the lover your partner deserves, you must ask yourself:

"How well does my touch speak
the language of love?"
and . . .
**"What has my touch been saying
to my partner?"**

Whether you've been aware of it or not, the way you touch your partner has been sending a silent but powerful energetic message into his or her body. Perhaps your touch has been saying one of the following:

"Hurry up and get turned on . . . I hope this doesn't take long."

"I don't care about what makes you feel good—The way I'm doing this right now makes me feel good."

"I'm embarrassed doing this to you."

"I don't feel the way I used to about you."

If you can't figure out what your touch has been saying, ask your partner to tell you what he or she feels it's been saying. Naturally, your lover's response will be different at different times. Be open to what you hear, even if it hurts. And be honest with yourself about what you've been feeling inside during lovemaking, and why your mate might be feeling the way he does.

How to Practice Loving Touch

The first step in touching your partner with love is to *find the love you feel for him or her inside your-self.* You might take a moment before you begin to make love, close your eyes, and think about how much you care for this wonderful person. Focus your awareness on all of the things you adore about him, all of the joy she has brought into your life. Don't get trapped in your mind's collection of hidden grievances or list of imperfections—**this isn't the time to concentrate on what's wrong with your partner (a sure turn-off), but rather, to remind yourself what is right about her.**

Once you feel the love for your partner in your heart, **the second step in practicing loving touch is to move the love energy from your heart into your hands.** Here are several techniques you can use to achieve this. Try these, or create your own:

✦ *Rivers of Love*

Feel your love for your mate in your heart like a powerful ocean. Visualize the water as clear, sparkling, and silver. Then, imagine two rushing rivers flowing down into your hands from the center of that sparkling ocean of love in your chest. Feel the force of all that love vibrating in your hands, on your fingertips. As you begin touching your partner's body, imagine those powerful rivers of love energy pouring from the ocean in your heart through your hands and into your beloved.

✦ Rivers of Fire

Imagine that the love and desire you feel for your partner is like a fire that burns strong and hot in your heart. Feel the flames of passion and longing flickering inside you, and visualize them red and glowing. These are not flames that are dangerous and cause harm—they are flames that create excitement in whatever they touch. Then, imagine that the fire from your heart spreads down your arms and into your hands. Feel the heat and passion radiating from your hands and fingertips. As you begin touching your lover's body, imagine the heat and desire passing from your hands into your partner, igniting the flesh with pleasure, igniting his heart with joy.

✦ Rivers of Light

Find the love you feel for your partner as a sensation of fullness in your heart, and imagine that feeling as a beautiful, dazzling light. You can see the light as white, golden, rose-colored, or whatever color seems right. Visualize your heart filled with that light, like a shining sun overflowing with love. Now imagine the powerful light in your heart flowing like two dazzling rivers, spreading down your arms and into your hands. Feel your hands and fingertips tingling with that beautiful light, and when you touch your partner, imagine the light from your hands passing into his or her body, illuminating it with love.

Touching With Reverence in the Moment

One of the reasons we often get sidetracked from touching with love is that *we focus too much on what body part we are touching and how quickly we can turn it on rather than how we are touching it and who it belongs to.* "I'm touching a breast. Gosh, how exciting! Maybe if I do this to it, she'll get turned on faster," you think to yourself. There's nothing wrong with paying attention to what your hand is touching, or wanting to make it feel good, but you'll be tempted to just love that breast or that thigh or that belly as an erotic object, and forget about *whose* breast or thigh or belly it is. **You'll be having sex with a body—you won't be making love to a person.**

*A*lways touching your partner with
the sole purpose of turning her on
can not only cut you off from your
emotions, but inevitably, it will pull you
out of the moment.

When you focus too much on trying to turn your lover on, you will miss the real moment you're experiencing right now. You'll see touching as *foreplay,* something you do before the "real thing," rather than as a loving activity in itself. This is why many of us rush through preintercourse lovemaking—we're trying to get foreplay "out of the way." The result is that we miss those moments of love and intimacy that ultimately would make physical union so much more powerful and pleasurable.

The best real moments you can experience during touching occur when you're **touching your lover without being goal oriented,** without looking for or expecting certain results. You are focusing all of your awareness on what you are doing *when* you're doing it. I call this *touching with reverence.*

> *T*ouching with reverence means
> focusing your attention on
> the person inside the flesh,
> making love to her heart and soul,
> not just her body.

✦ *Touching With Reverence*

Imagine that your partner is the most beautiful, precious being in the world, the embodiment of everything you need, God's greatest gift to you. Approach her body *not as flesh that you want to turn on, but as a part of her you want to worship.* Reach out and begin to touch her as you would a priceless treasure, slowly, carefully, with reverence.

As your hands travel across her body, keep your mind and heart focused on that attitude of worship: *"I am touching the thing I love and cherish the most."* Don't think about certain body parts as more exciting or erotic than others. Let your lover's body become like an exquisite living statue, a sacred piece of art that you feel honored to adore.

Even as your partner becomes aroused, *don't rush out of the moment you are in.* Don't focus on what you want her to feel in the next moment—focus on loving her completely in *this* moment. You have all the time in the world . . .

When you touch with reverence, silently remind yourself:

"My purpose is not to turn my partner on. My purpose is to love her right now, in this moment."

✦

How will your lover feel when you touch her with reverence? She will feel like you are worshipping her, like every part of her is equally beautiful and equally desirable. *She will feel like a goddess.* She will feel more loved by you than she has ever felt before, and even though it's not what you are focusing on, she will become more physically excited than you've ever seen her. Why? Because your love is penetrating through her flesh, turning on the deepest places in her heart and soul. Because she can *feel* you there with her, fully, completely, in the moment.

Greedy Touch and Giving Touch

Some of us touch our lovers with the intention of turning *ourselves* on, rather than expressing our love for our partner through our hands. I call this **greedy touch** — the opposite of the loving, giving touch we've been talking about. **Your hands aren't giving off love energy, but are grabbing sexual energy from your partner for your own pleasure.**

When you are touching someone with greedy touch, you are focused on pleasuring yourself and not him or her. As your hands move over your partner's body, your mind is thinking: *"Look at these breasts! They are really getting me excited. Now I'm touching her thigh — this is really turning me on!!"*

Greedy touch cuts you off from your lover and isolates you in your own world of self-stimulation. *It's as if you are using your partner's body only to stimulate your own.* And how is your partner feeling when you are touching her with greedy touch? She's probably feeling used, disconnected, and frustrated since she can't possibly catch up with your level of sexual arousal.

*I*t's not *what* you do with your hands
that will determine whether your touch
is greedy or giving.
It's the *intention behind* the touch.

You can be the most physically skilled lover in the
world, but if you're touching your partner in order to
satisfy only yourself she won't feel much at all. Remember, it's not what you're doing that turns her on—it's the
energy from your hands, and *when none of your love energy is flowing out, but you're sucking energy in, you become
like a "sexual energy vampire."*

Take turns with your lover practicing greedy and giving touches on each other when you're not planning to
actually make love:

Close your eyes, and choose one type of touch. When
you choose *greedy* touch, do the same things with your
hand and fingers that you'd ordinarily do, but imagine
that your hand is like a vacuum cleaner, sucking up all
the energy from your partner's body. When you choose
giving touch, use the techniques I suggested earlier in this
chapter. See if your lover can feel the difference between
greedy and giving touch, and guess which one you're
using. You'll be surprised at what a difference your intention makes, and how much more powerful and sexually exciting giving touch is, not just for the person
you're touching, but for you as well.

♦

Your hands hold a magical power. They can give the passion in your soul a voice. They can speak of things for which there are no words. They can make your love visible.

**$\mathcal{L}$ike an artist molding figures
out of clay,
your hands, as they touch,
give shape and form to your devotion,
so that your beloved might know
how much he or she is loved.**

Use your touch to worship the sacred temple of your
    lover's body. . . .
Use your touch to sing your lover's praises. . . .
Use your touch to say what words can never say. . . .

Use your touch to love.

8

Kissing: Sharing the Breath of Life

*S*omehow, it is not enough to hold him, to touch him, to feel your lover's body pressed against yours. You long for more. You are hungry to taste him, to nibble on his lips, to lose yourself in his mouth. *It is time for a kiss.*

Kissing is one of the most intimate sexual acts you can experience. When you place your mouth on the mouth of the person you love, you are sharing the very essence of life—your breath. It is your breath that sustains your existence in this physical body. It is your breath that sends oxygen to your brain, so it can think and feel and live.

*W*hen you share your breath
with your beloved,
you are offering him your most sacred
and necessary treasure.

Breath was your first link to life, and it will be your last. In the womb your mother breathed for you. Then, as soon as you were born, you greedily tasted your first gulp of air. You were alive!

In this way, breath was your first food, and still is your most important one. *That is why sharing your breath is one of the most meaningful acts of love there is — you are sharing the very food that gives you life.*

Sharing food is a very ancient and primal form of love. From the beginning of time, sharing food bound people together in tribes, in families, as mates. So kissing and sharing breath, the food of life, binds you and another person together.

Instinctively, we know this. At times in our life, we let casual lovers see us naked, touch us, even enter or receive us, but perhaps we did not let them really kiss us, or we did not kiss them. Intimate kissing would have forced us closer together and made our brief encounter much more meaningful, and we didn't want that to happen.

Thus, the passionate kiss stands alone, even above intercourse, as an act in which both lovers are

equally open to one another. Each offers the other that which is sacred, each receives the sacrament back. We may think we're just smooching, but in truth, our souls are breathing together.

Feasting on the One You Love

Human beings are very oral creatures—we love to put things in our mouths, even things we don't need like: lollipops, toothpicks, gum, hard candies, pipes, cigarettes, cigars, fingernails . . . the list goes on. Once the object is inserted into our oral cavity, we contentedly chew, suck, gnaw, nibble, and munch to our heart's delight.

Of course, the substance we enjoy putting in our mouths the most is food. Next to sex, there's no human pleasure as enjoyable as eating (although some people have the importance of these reversed). *When you combine your need to eat with your need to love, you have: kissing!*

*K*issing is really your way of chewing,
sucking, gnawing, nibbling, and
munching on that which you cherish
the most, your mate.
It is a form of "eating" the person
you love!!

When we think of the kiss as what comes before the really fun sexual stuff, we miss the opportunity to feast on the person we love. The purpose of a kiss is not to get your partner "ready"—it is to experience your One-ness right now. ***A kiss is not a pit stop on the way to orgasm, but a total communion in itself.***

✦

Your partner's mouth is a doorway into his or her being. *In this way, the act of kissing imitates the act of sexual intercourse.* A part of you enters your partner's body, a part of you receives his or her body into yours.

When you approach the door of your lover's physical home, whether it is his mouth, or during inter-course, your woman's sexual opening, don't forget to display your best manners: *Always knock gently, and wait until you are invited in to enter.*

If you are kissing, allow your lips and your tongue to approach your partner's mouth with respect—do not let your tongue barge right in. Let your lips quietly say hello, until you feel your lover opening to receive you. If you are looking for an invitation into your woman's vagina, this same courtesy should apply—*let your mouth, fingers, or penis approach her sacred opening slowly and with reverence.* You'll end up being invited in much faster this way, and, once you are inside, you'll find a much happier and more grateful body waiting to greet you.

Kissing With Love

Like touching, it is the *intention behind your kiss that will determine whether your lover thinks the kiss is slimy or sublime.* **If you are connected to the love you feel for your partner, and allow that love to flow from your heart and into your lips and tongue, your kiss will transmit that love energy into the mouth of your beloved.** But if you are disconnected from your feelings, and kiss your partner mainly to turn yourself on, or to get the kissing out of the way so you can proceed to intercourse as quickly as possible, your mouth and tongue will be treated like unfriendly and unappealing invaders forcing their way into your lover's mouth.

The same techniques I offered you for loving touch in Chapter Seven can also all be used to create the sweetest and most satisfying of kisses.

Instead of imagining the love flowing from your heart down into your hands, **feel all your desire and devotion moving up from your heart into your mouth until your lips and tongue are vibrating with love.** Imagine that with each kiss, you are caressing your lover's mouth with that love. Feel your love flowing from your mouth into the mouth of your partner.

Tell yourself, "I am not just kissing the mouth of my beloved—I am kissing her heart and soul."

You can use the Rivers of Love, Fire, or Light, or the technique for Touching with Reverence to infuse your kisses with more passion and emotion.

✦

*K*isses are blessings you offer
your lover.
Wherever you place your mouth
on your partner's body,
your love consecrates that space
and your breath blesses the flesh.

Wherever your kisses take you as they travel over your lover's body, imagine yourself planting little blessings, honoring that forehead, that breast, that belly, that foot, that sexual organ, as your mouth worships the physical form of your most beloved.

Kiss your lover, and let your mouth make love to hers . . .

Kiss your lover as if that is all you are allowed to do, and let it be enough . . .

Kiss your lover, and let each kiss be a sharing of souls as the breath of life dances between you. . . .

9

When Bodies Unite and Souls Dance

Here is the truth about sex: The physical aspect of sexual union, the rubbing and panting and pressing and pleasuring that we all so desperately crave, even the great thundering orgasm we seek, *that is just the beginning of what sex is all about.* **Sex as it should be starts where your bodies unite, and ends where your souls dance, in a place where there is no ending.** This is the journey that awaits you when you choose to travel the path of High Love, and when you use the sexual experience as an opportunity for sacred communion.

Not many of us have explored sexual union and the power it has to transform us physically, emotionally, and spiritually. We live in a modern-day Western civilization that is still learning, and slowly at that, to be comfortable with the physical part of sex—we haven't even considered that something far greater than "good sex" awaits us. Instead, we focus on using sex for pleasure and miss out on the real magic that sexual union can create.

Some of the most exquisite real moments you and your lover can share together will happen when you begin to explore sex as a *physical celebration of the spiritual.* The play of your bodies becomes the platform upon which the cosmic life force can express itself in you, between you, surrounding you. Where you once experienced pleasure during lovemaking, now you will know true ecstasy.

These experiences are not out of your reach. They are not only available for people who have spent a long time studying Eastern lovemaking techniques. *Sacred sex is the true nature of the sexual ritual, and to begin experiencing it, all you need to do is open up to more real moments of love.*

> The real moments in our lovemaking happen where the sex leaves off and the love begins.

✦

When you unite your body with the body of your lover, you create the potential for great joy or great sorrow. That is the risk in such a powerful act:

. . . If your bodies are intimately connected, but your hearts are not, you may feel more empty when you are finished than you did before.

. . . If your partner makes love to your body, but forgets about your spirit, you may feel angry or ashamed.

. . . If you open your body to your lover, but he doesn't open his heart to you, you may feel used and wounded.

It is not enough that you and your lover be good sexual partners. You must be surrendered to loving each other, and being loved by each other while your bodies are playing. *Love is always necessary to transform sex from a physical act to a sacred ritual that will deepen your relationship.*

All sexual intercourse should
culminate in an act of creation—
it should give birth to more love.
That is why we call it *making* love.

Many lovers only experience glimpses of the sacred during their lovemaking: the sudden sensation that the boundaries between yourself and your lover have melted away, and you are One; the realization, during a surge of great passion, that you can't feel where your body stops and where your partner's begins; the moment during orgasm when you feel as if you are pulsating with the eternal rhythms of the Universe.

We often attribute these "natural highs" to the great sex we were having at the time. But in reality, they have nothing to do with the sex itself. **These spiritual experiences occur because, in each case, something happens that forces you totally into present time, and therefore, forces you to have a real moment.** You stop thinking about what experience you *want* to have, and simply surrender to *what is already happening* right then.

The moment you let go of control, you feel a powerful energy greater than yourself, greater than your partner, greater than the two of you. It is boundless, timeless, bliss—it is the life force, the very Source of everything.

You may be thinking to yourself, "That sounds like what I experience when I have an orgasm—I lose myself into something greater, something utterly ecstatic." If you're like most people, it's probably only during orgasm that you fully surrender into the moment, so you only experience that cosmic high for a few seconds. **But you don't have to wait until you reach orgasm to have this kind of orgasmic experience.**

When you learn to remain
fully in the moment,
opening yourself
to the powerful energies dancing
between you and your partner,
lovemaking becomes
a continually orgasmic process.

Finding Real Moments During Sexual Union

You and your lover must find your own way to each other during sexual union, and ultimately, to your own real moments of energy ecstasy. If you need them, there are many excellent books that can serve as very detailed and technical guides to a spiritual sexual experience. My purpose here is not so much to fully instruct you as it is to begin expanding your vision and opening your heart to a more complete, sacred kind of love. And for that, you need to create more real moments.

◆

✦ *Staying in the Moment*

When sex is about reaching a goal, you will miss out on the moments that could transform it into true love-making. You will be too busy trying to turn your partner on, or trying to have an orgasm, or trying to make your sexual encounter match some fantasy picture you have in your head of how sex "should" be. You're focused on what you *want* to happen, so you can't fully experience what *is* happening.

*I*f you are in a hurry
to get somewhere during sex,
you'll miss the experience of
where you are,
and you'll never know the
real moments of timeless ecstasy
that are waiting for you
if only you'd pay attention to NOW.

Rushing toward orgasm is one of the ways we prevent ourselves from being continually orgasmic. If you don't know what I'm talking about, try slowing way down when you make love. **When you feel the sexual energy building up in your body, don't race ahead to push yourself over the edge into orgasm.**

Instead: PAUSE . . . BREATHE . . . Allow your body to become accustomed to the intensity of the physical sensation before you begin moving again. It may seem like you're doing nothing. But if you let your awareness sink deeper into the silence between your movements, and focus on the love energy flowing between you and your partner, rather than on your own arousal, you will find yourself melting into the Oneness.

When you're ready, you can begin moving together again. *You'll find that you're now able to handle even more pleasure and stimulation without feeling that you need to release it,* and that the waves just keep getting bigger and bigger.

The better you get at staying in the moment, and the longer you allow the sexual energy to circulate in your body before releasing it, the greater your physical and emotional ecstasy will become.

✦ *Making Love from the Heart*

Even more than during a caress or a kiss, *it is what you are feeling in your heart, and not what you are doing with your body, that creates the real and ecstatic moments during sexual union.* If you appreciated the importance of kissing and touching with reverence as I previously described it, you will understand that having intercourse with reverence is the *only* way you and your partner can ascend into a higher state of sexual experience together. It is your love alone that will make it safe enough for your partner to let go of control and surrender into the cosmic energy that flows between you.

What Women Can Do to Make a Man Feel Loved During Intercourse

When a man enters a woman, he can sense the places inside of her that aren't willing to fully receive him, the places where he isn't welcome. Even though he may be penetrating you physically, part of him will feel psychically rejected or turned away. Most men won't be conscious of this awareness at all, but their unconscious sense of it might manifest in their "hurrying up" the act so they can get out quickly, or pulling back their love so that you end up perceiving him as detached or distant.

As a woman, your blocks to fully receiving your man may have to do with your fear of being too vulnerable, or the way you've been hurt in the past by other men, or simply a fear of letting someone that deeply into your being. **The more welcome you can make your man feel when he is inside of you, the more powerful your emotional connection will be, and the higher you'll both get.**

When you are about to receive your man inside your body, visualize yourself opening with joy. Think to yourself, *"All of me welcomes all of you, my beloved. I receive all you bring into me, I receive everything you have to offer."* Imagine your body surrounding your partner with beautiful, golden light and see the light spreading until it reaches out to cover him in an aura of safety and love. Feel your body drinking in the energy essence of this man you love, welcoming all of him with joy and celebration.

What Men Can Do to Make a Woman Feel Loved During Intercourse

When a woman receives a man into her body, she can sense that there are parts of you that did not arrive along with your penis, the parts of your heart and soul you aren't willing to share. It is painful for a woman to open herself in such a vulnerable way to your body, knowing all the while that the rest of you hasn't shown up. Although she may not be aware that she's feeling this way, she will be filled with an unidentified loneliness or sadness— *she's missing your true spirit.* This can cause her body to remain tense, or to have a difficult time achieving orgasm, or simply leave her anxious and emotionally oversensitive.

> *A* woman needs to feel she is
> penetrating her man emotionally
> in the same way that he is
> penetrating her physically.

Just as it's important for you as a man to feel fully received by your woman during intercourse, so she needs to feel you're receiving her emotionally, that you're bringing all of yourself to her. **The more you let yourself surrender into your love for her, without holding anything back, the more love you will both feel, and the higher you'll both get.**

When you are about to enter the woman you love, visualize *all of your being* flowing into her with joy and anticipation. Think to yourself, *"My beloved, I bring all of myself to you. Feel all of me here with you, moving into the sacred space of your womb. I honor you for receiving me."* See yourself surrounded with beautiful, golden light, and see that light entering her body, spreading your love and adoration up into her heart, until it covers all of her. Imagine as you penetrate her body, her love is penetrating your heart, as if you are receiving her inside yourself as well.

✦

Do not underestimate the power of these techniques. They will open your heart to your beloved, and open your beloved's heart to you.

*W*hen the channel between
your two hearts is unblocked,
your spirits can join together
at the same time as your bodies
become one.
Then all of you will be making love,
and there will be nothing left between
you that is not love.
This is sacred communion.
This is ecstasy.

✦

This, then, is how it should be . . .
You lie together,
   melting into each other,
   melting into the love that is your Source,
   melting into all that is.
You are the eternal male and female.

All of creation rejoices through you.
All of creation loves through you.
   You are everything.
   You are everywhere.
You have come home. . . .

SEMINARS WITH
BARBARA DE ANGELIS, Ph.D.

All of Barbara De Angelis's books have been inspired by the experiences of thousands of people who have undergone a powerful emotional transformation after attending her workshops and seminars. Barbara is highly sought after for lectures, conferences and speaking engagements throughout the world, and in her own unique, dynamic and entertaining style, uplifts and motivates her audiences on the topics of love, relationships and personal growth.

If you would like to receive a schedule of Barbara's seminars in your area, or contact her to set up an event, please call or write:

Barbara De Angelis Seminars
12021 Wilshire Boulevard
Suite 607
Los Angeles, CA   90025
Phone: (310) 820-6600
Fax: (310) 820-4478